Deep Waters

Volume 1

Sean R. E. Munnings

LMH

LMH Publishing Limited

Cover Design: *Lee-Quee Design*

Editor: *Kevin S. Harris*

Design & Typesetting: *PAGE Services*

Published by: LMH Publishing Limited
7 Norman Road,
LOJ Industrial Complex
Building 10
Kingston C.S.O., Jamaica
Tel: 876-938-0005; 938-0712
Fax: 876-759-8752
Email: lmhbookpublishing@cwjamaica.com
Webside: www.lmhpublishingjamaica.com

Printed in U.S.A.   ISBN: 976-8184-74-4

Acknowledgements

Parents (Ruis and Ingrid Munnings), Brothers (Damien, Eathon and Rommel), Ophelia Munnings and the Munnings family, Joy Kikivarakus, Simone Blackwood and the White family, Eric Rose, Giovanni Stuart, Granville Weech, Duane T. Knowles, Natasha Dean, Cohen Johnson, Tanya L. Thompson, Colleen Williams, Winnifred Russell, Dandria Scott, Monty Kohli, Percival Galloway, Leanette Gore, Shavonne Lockhart, Corey and Tracee Rolle-Lightbourne, Nicole McDonald, Urvan Moxey, Jeffrey Sturrup, Karen Edie, Nathalie Wood, Sheila Cherizard, Darlyne Cange, Kim Taylor, Kevin & Tammy Cambridge, Jeunesse Osadebay, Vanessa Taylor, Carol Scriven, Erald Thompson, Lynette Major, Ingrid Culmer, The employees of PricewaterhouseCoopers (Bahamas), The employees of Dartley Bank & Trust Limited, The Crew from Krissy Luv's Speakeasy, Koumbah Creativity, The Verse Place, Generation Blessed, Toastmaster Club 7178, Chapel on the Hill, Teachers of Queen's College Class of 1989, The University of South Florida Caribbean Cultural Exchange and Club Creole.

Preface

With clear-headed simplicity, Sean Munnings delves into the heart of our deepest feelings and secret thoughts. As a native Bahamian with Guyanese and British heritage, he embraces his cultures and addresses a myriad of subjects. Many of the poet's friends and family recognized his unique talent and gift to communicate passionately and expose a wide variety of human emotions. From the age of thirteen he had started to develop this strength. His ability to honestly convey the deepest thoughts makes reading his work enjoyable and satisfying.

"Deep Waters Volume I" is a journey that extends into the joys, despairs and passions of life. His writing is direct, uncompromising and sincere. This book offers a practical look at community and individual ideals, moral compromises and challenges faced in everyday life. Best of all, Sean Munnings dares us as a community and as individuals to question our beliefs, values and actions. His rare blend of creative talent and clarity engages mature audiences everywhere to look at societal and personal issues. His remarkable sensitivity to circumstances that affect both sexes is extraordinary.

I recommend that as you dive into "Deep Waters Volume I", that you take time to explore the hidden treasures buried here. The poems in this volume are drawn out of the poet's beliefs and sensitivity, cultural biases and social influences. Indulge your mind and spirit on an adventure into an ocean of romance, conflict, and human aspirations.

Dandria Scott

Introduction

The Bahamas is an archipelago of islands with powder-white and conch-shell pink beaches, crystal clear waters, hidden depths and shallow shores. Added to these wondrous attributes, the most vibrant resource is its people. With this in mind, I have compiled a collection of poems that paint a picture of my experiences and thoughts as a native living in the Bahamas. What has emerged is a candid perspective on popular and unpopular behavior, ideas and experiences.

As a child, I began writing poetry to express thoughts that seemed difficult to convey ordinarily. Adopting the pen name, the Raga~Lover, my initial subjects focused mostly on romance then expanded to other themes. I have always desired the gift to create memorable lyrics such as those penned by Dianne Warren, Kenny "Babyface" Edmonds and Lionel Richie. I have found writing poetry to be an outlet that addresses the core of an issue and exhibits the exact emotions associated with it. With constant encouragement from my parents, Ruis and Ingrid Munnings, I was able to experiment and develop a style of my own.

"Deep Waters Volume I" represents a collage of rhythmic verses I have developed over the years. My basic intent is that these lyrics will provoke feelings and thoughts regarding the choices we make in life. My objective is to utilize common words to depict the harsh reality of subject matter which society considers taboo. The purpose of this book is to not only to entertain, but also to open the minds of all readers.

Contents

The Bahamas
Bahamian time
There go the lights
Someone (Election Day 1992)
Food for the soul (Junkanoo music)
How long
This land

Pearls of Purity

*W*hen all of my accomplishments are said and done,
I want to be remembered as my Father's son.
In times of crisis you have been my best friend,
in confusion's darkness you've been my guiding light.
Conveying wisdom and responsibility to a teenager,
who once believed that youth could overcome any plight.
Many times I strayed from the path of righteousness,
but as a role model, your actions showed me the way.
It's because of you, that I am willing to seek
an abiding relationship with Jesus today.
I was spoiled with your love, admonished by your belt.
Molded into a man by your friendship
and educated with your wealth.
This son of God is truly blessed to have been placed in your care.
Any gifts my mother lacked,
you were always willing to share.
Someday I hope to be a dedicated husband, like you,
and raise a family.
Nurture and support a daughter or son
who will be my living tribute to society.
Look into my child's face;
see my reflection smiling back at me.
Marvel in delight every time I hear him or her say, "Daddy."
Many fathers give their money, or their name;
but you gave the best part.
Dad, you gave your time, your understanding,
and most importantly your heart.

I Will Never Do

I t hurts when a cherished one
does not wish to be solely
committed to you;
because he deems you to be too perfect,
too virtuous to be true.
I don't play devilish mind games;
I don't take the pill.
Although I might have felt like cheating on him;
I never did, and I never will.
So it is another five years for me he says,
until he has satisfied his lust for another.
But it is not my fault that I was taught to exercise
physical restraint by my mother.
Drunkardness, promiscuity and profanity
are against my moral code.
That means that I have to travel
a very lonely road.
He thinks that I will be waiting for him
after he sows his royal oats.
I will wait, but not for him;
because he has missed this beautiful boat.
To him, I am too perfect, too virtuous to be true.
I am the girl that he would wish to marry,
and that is why I will never do.

Draw Me Towards You

Draw me towards you like the moon and the tide.
Take this wanton soul
on a magic carpet ride.
Pull me towards you like a magnet and steel.
Bring life to this wooden puppet
and allow me to feel.
Entice me towards you like a bear to honey.
Dare me to sell my possessions,
calm my desire for money.
Attract me towards you like a bee to a flower.
Never allow my fears and my expectations
to hinder your power.
Draw me towards you like a fish to bait.
Never allow me to lose my faith.

Like Strays

*I*t is hard to not sleep around,
and be faithful day after day.
To be honest and truthful,
while the others run around like strays.
But the more I practice to be different,
the easier it becomes.
Hence, the less baggage I have to carry
when trouble comes.
Not to drink, not to smoke,
not to purchase pornography or spout profanity.
Not to surround myself with such demonic thoughts;
allowing them to become a part of me.
I read my Bible when I am discouraged;
I cast my burdens upon the Lord.
I always look towards greener pastures,
never spending more than I can afford.
Although I am not a diligent churchgoer,
I am a humble servant of my faith.
My parents will never have to be ashamed
of the son they helped create.
An unplanned pregnancy will never be found
knocking at my door.
I will never vomit from intoxication
and collapse on the floor.
My lover will never have to wonder
where my behind was last night.
I would sacrifice my pride (even if I'm right)
in order to quash a fight.
Some guys will deem me to be less than a man,
but I don't care what they say!
As I will continue to be honest and trustworthy,
while they run around like strays.

Show Me The Way

Lord, take me by the hand, show me the way.
I'm just a wayward child,
trying to follow your footsteps everyday.
I read your word,
its teachings I store readily in my heart.
But there are so many interpretations
of what you said by Bible scholars,
that it's ripping me apart.
I love you dear Jehovah,
your commands I promise to obey.
Master take me by the hand, and show me the way.
Heavenly Father, this child who was made
in your image wants so much to follow you.
Help me overcome all obstacles that try to hinder me
from doing what you want me to do.
Satan plagues my mind with a cloud of confusion,
that only you can make go away.
My friend, take me by the hand, show me the way.
Let your spirit in me, guide me,
and may I never go astray.
Help me to be worthy of being in your presence,
when you reveal yourself to me
in heaven someday.

Love Me for Me

Love me for me, look past the expensive clothes
I can buy.
Love me for me, not for the shoulder
that comforts you
when you cry.
Love me for me, look past the car that I drive in.
Love me for me, not for the trinkets in life
that I have managed to win.
Love me for me, not for the degrees on my wall.
Love me for me, not because I am always there
to embrace you when you fall.
Love me for me, not because of the lavish sums
of money I spend.
Love me for me, look past the gifts and the flowers
I frequently send.
Love me for me, not for the romantic things
I write or say.
Love me for me; allow my actions to show you the way.
Love me for me, not because I always make you
feel good.
Love me for me, the way a lover and a friend should.
Love me for me, not when everything is rosy in your life.
Love me for me, in times of bitterness, heartache
and strife.
Woman, there is more to this man
than what your eyes can see.
A heart, a mind and a soul that needs you to
love me for me.

Tides
of
Doubt

Another Lame Apology

*W*hy should I be the recipient of another lame apology?
I'm the woman; he should be waiting on me.
It's a quarter after eight, and I am home alone;
waiting anxiously for a knock at the door
or a ring of the telephone.
My makeup is running from the silent tears that fall.
I stare at the ceiling for an hour
and he still doesn't call.
I can't believe that he has done it again!
The clock is ticking and it is a quarter after ten.
Here he comes with no flowers or candy in his hands;
delivering an explanation
that is as solid as a patch of quicksand.
Utilizing his charm, and pleading with his puppy dog eyes.
Twitching his ear, especially when he lies.
I reply by declaring that our torrid relationship is history;
because I refuse to be the recipient of another lame apology.

S he sees forever, you see today.
To you, she is a fish in the sea,
the catch of the day.
She's thinking of marriage,
she believes that you are the one.
You believe that she's a nice girl who is a lot of fun.
She sees a lifetime commitment,
someone to comfort her when she's old.
You see a woman, one of many that you have had the
opportunity to hold.
She pours out her heart to you in letters and
burns the telephone line.
You see others,
but you manage to keep her hooked
with your candy-coated words,
guilty gifts and "miss you signs."
She caresses in affection, each stroke conveys her love for "only" you.
You touch to conquer, you kiss to subdue.
She sheds her undergarments with passion,
utter devotion she strives to profess.
You initiate petting to arouse and foreplay to undress.
She proclaims you to be her boyfriend based upon your actions;
but your chauvinistic pride merely sees "the temporary"
physical attraction.
She's thinking of marriage, she believes that you are the one;
and you will tell her what she wants to hear
as long as you can "hit and run."

Teddy Bear

No matter how intimate you become,
or how much he cares;
you will never make him fulfilled,
you will always be his teddy bear.
He will never dream of you, he will never give his all.
You think that the two of you are so close;
but you are too blind to see "the wall."
You are just someone to keep him warm,
to keep the loneliness at bay.
Someone to hold dear, while his true love lives far away.
During every cuddle his mind was not thinking about you.
Every kiss being dedicated to another woman,
but you never knew.
He can never honestly tell you that he loves you;
your presence only makes his life temporarily complete.
You're a tentative voice to speak to at night,
an available and cozy source of body heat.
Although you may have a special place in his heart,
and in his memories he holds you dear.
You will never make him fulfilled;
you will always be his teddy bear.

Love No More

*L*ove no more,
the day you threw me out,
and bolted the door.
Love no more,
the hour I lost the only thing in my life
worth living for.
I was stubborn and selfish,
and unwilling to listen, to learn.
Repeatedly ignoring your problems,
and replacing them with my own concerns.
So content to go out with the boys,
coming home in the wee hours of the night.
Leaving you alone in a big empty house,
with only a pillow to hold tight.
No compliments, just complaints, wanting only to eat,
work, drink, and sleep.
Unaware of the bad seed
that my actions had reaped.
You would always allow me to return to the house
after a fight.
As my shallow "good" intentions
would often set the situation right.
But this time nothing I can say or do
will persuade you to let me in.
Now I am learning what it is like to sleep alone,
tossing and turning.
Love no more,
the day you threw me out,
and bolted the door.
When the promise to be together
"until death do us part",
didn't matter to you anymore.

*O*ne bad decision destroyed my life.
One moment of weakness
caused me to lose the trust
of my wife.
I chose to risk our marriage
and to endanger my relationship with our child.
I chose to break my commitment to be faithful;
I chose to be "buck-wild".
I gambled with infidelity by playing Russian roulette
with a loaded gun.
I never thought it would happen to me, but now the deed is done.
Now I can't eat, I can't sleep,
as I'm immersed in a sea of self pity and sorrow.
Drowning without a forgiving family, without an abiding mistress,
without a reassuring promise of tomorrow.
Dying with no expectation of a ten-year anniversary date,
lost with no hope of ever seeing my baby graduate.
One bad decision has resulted in me contracting a lethal disease
that has no cure.
One moment of weakness and deception,
and my spouse changed all the locks on the doors.

Asking for My Man

*T*o break up my marriage is the goal of her plans;
calling my house at all hours asking for my man.
Who is this woman who dares
to mess with my mind?
Speaking to me with such candor as if I were a horse's behind.
Politely leaving a number for my husband to dial.
Acting courteous and considerate with words coated in bile.
Evading my questions as if she has something to hide.
Finally blurting out that my beloved is taking me for "a ride."
She adamantly states that this is a personal matter
between a husband and his wife.
Suddenly screaming as I threaten to come after her with a knife.
I cry as I curse her for being an adulteress and a whore.
She remains silent as I tell her that today she declared war.
I toss my wedding ring to the wall,
and slam the telephone as hard as I can.
Determined to physically confront this woman;
who dares to call my house asking for my man.

An Empty House

An empty house is the reason
she had to go away.
An empty house
is the reason
she refused to stay.
The house is quiet; the kitchen is bare.
He looks at the dining room and sees her house keys,
wedding ring and car keys lying there.
He heard what she said,
but her words he chose not to believe.
This was not the first time
that she has decided to leave.
For his attention, for his affection
she would have lived in a shack.
But this time he has an eerie feeling
that she won't be back.
He should have been receptive to her feelings,
but he didn't try.
Now she's reciprocating his actions
by not telling him good-bye.
An empty house is the reason
she had to go away.
An empty house is the reason
she refused to stay.

Smoking Gun

You shouldn't have fallen for me little one,
I'm not a dagger; I'm a smoking gun.
You should have hidden your trust,
your family jewels, and your heart from me.
Lust mistaken for love is an interlude to tragedy.
I am an experienced wolf,
able to undress and devour you.
I told you what I was when I met you,
but you deemed my words to be untrue!
I'm the type of man your mom, your aunt and your grand mother
told you to fear.
A dark angel who appears sincere,
but lacks the conscience to care.
Like a fish to bait
you failed to avoid this silent alluring shell.
Evidently becoming another victim
of my addictive petting spell.
When you begin to bore me
I will let you go.
Unlike many before you
I hope that you are able to withstand the blow.
You are a virgin snack before the dawn,
for this vampire to drain at night.
An innocent, cuddly teddy bear,
to toss aside or hold tight.
Like Eve in the Garden of Eden
you dared to provoke the powers that be.
Lust mistaken for love is an interlude to tragedy.
You shouldn't have fallen for me little one,
I'm not a dagger; I'm a smoking gun.

Shores
of
Matrimony

Angel Eyes

I was lost and alone
before I looked into
your angel eyes.
Convinced that my sun had set,
but you revealed to me "the sunrise."
A bright future in which I will not be condemned
to tarry along life's winding road alone.
Years of contentment and joy to
partake in the greatest love affair I've ever known.
Every burden of tomorrow lightened by
an extra shoulder of care,
through the valleys deep and mountain peaks
you will always be there.
And when this winding road comes to an end
and my spirit starts to soar;
thoughts of you will be with me
as I walk through death's dark door.
In you my memory will live on,
because our kind of love never dies.
And at heaven's gate,
I will rise again to look into your angel eyes.

Young hearts, young love, have you really thought it through?
Please give your engagement two more months
before you say I do.
I know you want the world to know
how much you love this person so;
but before you take a legal position
please take this relationship "a little slow."
Pure infatuation and sexual elation mistaken for love
can result in years of frustration.
Emotional sensations and mental contemplation
cannot guarantee a lifetime of dedication.
A marriage is a job that you have to constantly work at
for the rest of your life.
Be perfectly sure that you are ready to risk starting a family
before you become a husband or a wife.
Out of respect for your parents, I implore you to wait!
Learn to know yourself, mind, body and soul before it is too late.
A life long commitment is filled with joy, dedication,
hardship and pain.
It only takes one time, one mishap,
for a child to be conceived.
You curtail your freedom once you marry.
You limit your romantic love morally to only one.
Make sure that later in life that you won't have any regrets
after "the ceremony" is done.
Young hearts, young love, have you really thought it through?
No one can take responsibility for your life;
the decision is evidently up to you.

Happy Anniversary

*I*n our lives we create treasure chests
in which we store jewels
called memories;
and for a husband and wife the most
precious gem of them all
is their anniversary.
On that blessed day many years ago
two people made one promise to commit.
Thus two lives were irrevocably intertwined,
trust and security seeming infinite.
Through the hardships, the adversities, and the criticisms
you've persevered.
Your heartstring, your bond, resilient and prosperous
like a church built upon faith and prayer.
I wish that your love for each other is as rich and fulfilling
as the memories you both share;
and that you rekindle your passion and dreams anew
for another year.
As you revisit your treasure chest
to reflect on these sparkling memories true,
"Happy Anniversary," and love always from me to you.

The Vow

*T*his year I vow to be eternally true to you,
to give myself unequivocally in
every thing we do.
To no longer hold back those secret fantasies
I have discretely hidden inside.
To reveal each scintillating wave steadily to your shore
like the morning tide.
Like the tender buds of spring, I am prepared to blossom anew.
To greet everyday expectantly like the morning dew.
Burn with a fiery passion and desire like the summer sun.
Explore new exciting horizons beyond life's deepest ocean.
Fall gracefully in love again and again
like autumn leaves to the earth.
Keep my eyes on my goal, our goal,
in the midst of disappointment and hurt.
Tarry through the merciless winter;
seek comfort in your arms from the cold.
Shower compliments and gifts upon you,
the wondrous treasure I hold.
Promise to be faithful to our relationship as a captain to his crew.
Renew my resolution, my vow,
to be eternally true to you.

This Ring

*T*his ring
is a symbol of
my commitment
to one man, and only one man, forever.
It is a tribute to love everlasting,
a bond that only God alone may sever.
Around your neck for friendship,
around your finger for love.
Destined to fit your hand,
made to order like a silk glove.
Hence my darling, I give my mind and body
wholeheartedly to you.
To comfort in matrimony
as a lover ought to do.
When I was younger I prayed to God
that he would make an angel mine.
And during the day I would search the blue sky
for that heavenly sign.
So today I thank him
for bringing you into my life,
and for bestowing upon me the distinct honor
of being your wife.

The aisle

A veil of sadness overwhelms me
as she walks down the aisle.
It takes all of my energy
to maintain some semblance of a smile.
I remember all of the laughter,
all the tender embraces we shared.
Although we never discussed marriage,
we knew how much the other cared.
We were both committed to another then,
both living a temporal dream.
Both inscribing upon each other's heart
the other person's name.
It seems like an eternity passes by,
as she looks me in the eye.
I snap a photo of her with my camera
so that she doesn't see me cry.
As she tells him I do, she is telling me good-bye.
Consecrating the fact that I allowed a treasure
of affection to pass me by.
I excuse myself from the pew;
this is more than my body can take.
As I hear the words, "You may now kiss the bride,"
my trembling heart breaks.
As the happy couple joyously exits the aisle;
it takes all of my energy
to maintain some semblance of a smile.

Bear My Name

For once I can touch
what my heart
deemed only a dream.
A woman who is willing to live with me forever
and bear my name.
Woman, you don't know how long I have waited
for you to walk into my life.
Someone I can grow old and gray with,
someone to be my wife.
Darling, together we will soon be starting
a family of our own.
And it is so comforting, so heart warming,
to know that I will never be alone.
I am truly blessed by God
as he has allowed me the honor of knowing you.
And that ring on your finger
is a symbol of my commitment to this union of two.
My past, my old girlfriends, and my dating days
I have left behind, because I only have thoughts about one woman
on my mind.
I was a ship without an anchor,
drifting aimlessly until you came;
a lady who is willing to live with me forever
and bear my name.

Catastrophe

*W*hat do I do, what do we do, if he finds
out about you and me?
I'm his best man,
what a catastrophe that is going to be!
Woman, your voice is calling me, your words are paging me,
and your body has got me "whipped."
I'm an unrepentant sinner at the communion table
ready to face the "Almighty," break the "bread" and take a sip.
The wedding cake is on "ice," the church is decorated
and the rehearsal dinner is done.
You are having second thoughts and my mind is hinting at me
to leave your arms and run.
I can't even look my "bro" (my "boy") in the eyes no more;
every time he tells me how much he loves you
I want to head to the bathroom door.
Onion peels of guilt bring tears of shame
to my once trustworthy eyes.
Why did I not resist your charms
before becoming tangled in this web of lies?
My little head keeps saying yes,
my bigger head keeps saying, "I don't know."
Beneath your deep blue sea is the only place my thoughts, my loins
and my hands want to go.
My heart is torn between your twin reefs of confusion.
I wish to cover my ears and ignore fate's ugly conclusion.
Of all the women on this island,
why did I have to fall in love with you, his "lady?"
I'm his best man, what a catastrophe this is going to be!

Corals
of
Ebony

29

Sister, Please Forgive Me

ister, please forgive me, I didn't mean to make you cry.
Sister, I'm "so" sorry,
I never should have passed you by.
Like an egotistical hypocrite,
I've judged you by your color;
demeaning your worth and beauty to less than a dollar.
Choosing black rather than white;
to cater to my Nubian pride.
Choosing the lighter berries of the bunch,
before partaking of the persona inside.
How many times have I nearly broken my neck
to pursue the whiter meat;
forgetting that the darker portion is just as sweet?
Constantly walking into a room of strangers
and ignoring the fact that you are there.
My attention being vested completely in the mulatto,
mango skin girls with straight hair.
Although I personally prefer not to date a Caucasian,
I blatantly date someone just as bright.
Still afraid of my dark ancestral history,
still a mental prisoner of the light.
Teach me my friend, (a future father) that I may see through the
lies.
Teach me with a tempered voice
not to judge so quickly with my eyes.
Because I am just as selfish and naïve,
as the Europeans and settlers of old.
Just as blind to the truth, my actions being heartless and cold.
I am the Uncle Tom who delights in clearing his ebony name.
I am the problem, because I have never treated you the same.
Sister, please forgive me, I didn't mean to make you cry.
Sister, I'm "so" sorry, I never should have passed you by.

The Voice

(In Remembrance Of The Arsenio Hall Show.)

*T*he voice of the black man is bitter but true.
It is a constant reminder of the
racism and bigotry
that is hidden from view.
A wolf howling at the moon;
sending a chill of reality to open up eyes.
To show a future generation of minorities and others;
the goals and dreams they have yet to realize.
For now, that beautiful voice is gone,
condemned by the political rat race.
And in the darkness of late night there is no white substitute,
or Uncle Tom to take its place.
Someday, I hope to hear that illustrious voice again,
so that through him I may once again shine.
Because by curtailing the voice of the black man,
they want only smothered mine by design.
I will miss my intelligent, handsome brother,
because he looked like me.
I will miss my fine black brother
because he showed me where I ought to be.
He taught me to strive for diversity and equality
by refusing to be Hollywood's ebony pawn.
"Adeus, meu amigo,"
the voice of the black man on late night T.V. is gone.

She says that she doesn't love you.
But she enjoys your company;
so she treats you like a
second string fiddle.
How selfish can one black woman be?
To some you are the boyfriend;
to her you are just a friend.
A man with a glass label
and no future around the bend.
You are waiting on a star,
hoping that someday she will change her mind.
But that day will never come,
and she will inevitably leave you behind.
Still you continue to pursue her,
even though it has almost been a year.
Once again she says that she doesn't love you,
but this time you let her see your tears.
She only turns her head aside,
a reaction spurned by guilt.
Nevertheless you continue to seek her,
too blind to see the wall she has built.
She will only quietly dismiss you
when someone more alluring comes her way.
You're just a second string fiddle
which is only useful
when there is no finer instrument to play.

To The Key

To the black man, the one known as the key;
who searches for a woman,
a woman whom he believes to be
desperately empty.
To you that grasshopper of a man
who is not this sexy ant's type;
You will always be left knee high in the winter cold
craving after my (warm) bosom ripe.
For I am the black woman, I am the beautiful lock.
The cornerstone of the family, the relentless rock.
My hips are wide
and my valley of emotions run deep.
With these hands I've persevered even when the
corporate Neanderthal sleeps.
My temple is divine,
so don't you dare demean this body my dear;
because this is no female dog
or common garden tool that is standing before you
(no sir not here)!
From the beginning of time
I have been your ordained love,
and strongest weakness.
History books overflow with page after page
of how you have succumbed to me, the "sweetness."
So try your best my egotistical key,
try your best and be shocked.
Because it takes more than a simple twist and a turn
to open up this lock.

Hunger for the Light

I will persevere like tumble weed
until the woodcutter gives up the fight.
Until they realize that they are no
match for a people
who hunger for the light.
Although they may chop me to a stump,
my people and I shall never die.
Someday, some glorious day,
our branches, my branches, will touch and fill the sky.
My broad royal roots are the history, the religion, the music
and the folklore of my past.
Steadfast and strong with each strand of truth they secure me;
anchored with desire for wisdom that is destined to last.
In the midst of despair I stand tall,
my ebony bark always reaching upwards.
The more they stereotype me, the more they tell me I can't,
the more determined I am to strive forward.
The woodsman enslaved me with his technical fire,
fertilized me with his ivory education
and tried to make a flower garden out of me.
Told me in his institutions, his groves, that I could be like him;
and stretch towards the sun.
Proving only to appease his heightened conscious,
whilst poisoning my people with his Caucasian god,
processed drugs, and metal guns.
Even though my people were uprooted,
and purchased with ignorance from their native land;
I am now a part of this country
because of the fruits of labor my ancestors bore
to make this country grand.
The soil and the manure are my forefathers
who have suffered so that I may succeed.
With knowledge, dexterity and beauty they feed my planted seed.

The wretched rocks that hinder my success
are the single parent families, welfare programs,
and concrete slums.
But in the midst of utter confusion
and a thirst for a distinct culture,
my people still strive with a dream to overcome.
My people;
flashing their emerald leaves in the face of their oppressors,
always diligently hungering for the light.
Too beautiful, too black, too bountiful,
too bright to give up the fight.
Although many of the males of my people fight like angry weeds
and have lost their way.
In time they will learn to bear their equal burden of our families,
and forge a brighter day.
It is written that we were a part of this earth
before the woodcutters came.
And we are still different
even though most of us bear their European names.
The woodcutters' axes swing subtly with their laws,
and with each stroke my people are silently suffering,
waiting patiently until we have majority power
to administer our own healing.
To prevent our backs from peeling,
and to virtually stop our offspring from bleeding.
My people;
don't ever become too bogged down in your altered, stolen past,
or grovel in your apathetic disillusioned present
and seething pain. Diligently hunger for the light,
and cultivate a brighter tomorrow upon the branches of truth
and newfound respect that you have gained.

Make Me Remember

Lord; make me remember the way my forefathers bled.
Make me remember
that there was a price on each one's head.
Like the majority of my generation,
I have become lost in the shuffle of democracy;
ignorantly acting like racism and bigotry
does not apply to me.
My chocolate reflection is assassinated on television
and I'm stereotyped as a clown or a gangster
on the movie screen.
Positive attributes of my character and others like me
are rarely seen.
I am the victim of Caucasian oppression
in most books that I have read.
The corporate glass ceiling may be lower today
but it still towers over my head.
Lord; make me remember
the way each slave hung from the tree.
Make me remember the scars from the whips,
and the heavy shackles around each body.
Make me remember the rotten scraps they were left to eat.
Make me remember the singing, the dancing
and the Afro-centric beat.
I need to know in my heart the reason why I am free today.
Lord; make me remember the tar and feathers
so that I may tell my children someday.

I Am

I am poisoned by the white man's fears in his books,
and I am denounced by the white man's lies.
I am constantly troubled by my people's anger,
and my ears are never closed to their cries.
In desperation I seek a solution;
in a sinner's prayer from God above,
but He answers not my bloodstained request conceived of hatred,
and not of (Agape) love.
I am a prisoner of the mind; conformed to a drunken state,
and made to be content in my cell.
Lost in the darkness of my own wretched soul, a colored stone;
drowning at the very bottom of a pregnant well.
When I try to place my head above the turbid water,
an icy crystal ceiling keeps me at bay.
It reminds me of my history and culture that are scattered
like stale bread crumbs
for the birds of industry to consume each day.
Hence the persecution, slaughter, and defecation of my ancestors
grow and dwell inside.
And the stench quickens the stereotypes and prejudices
that I try so reluctantly to hide.
I can no longer use the white man as a crutch
for my own shortcomings and hardships.
And allow the poison to be passed from my veins,
and be marred upon a future generation's lips.
Red, yellow, tan, black, or white must accept the past
and build a new future in order for the confusion and racism to cease.
Instilling unity in each other, and unity in the whole,
practicing God's remedy of brotherly love and peace.

Seaweed
of
Confusion

Complication

*H*ow does she deal with the loneliness,
the constant alienation?
Why build up her hopes
only to be dumped
due to a complication?
The truth is that there are no line of guys at the door;
just the "straggler;" the "player;"
who only wants to "score."
Sometimes her self-esteem has been so low
that she has allowed two or three to get in.
Hoping that she could lick her wounds
and coat her scars with sexual healing.
Yet, she still walks around like damaged goods,
but inanimate objects don't bear hurt.
She has temporarily lost some of her youth
and discounted her self worth.
Time after time, (once her past is revealed)
she is rejected by "another."
She is a wonderful person
but all they see is a single mother.
She loves her child,
he is the abiding sunshine in her life;
but every guy who walks away
pokes and stabs at her like a knife.
Her prince will come someday
to set her free from her frustrations.
Someone who is willing to accept this passenger
and her baggage as a blessing;
and not dump her due to a complication.

I Joined to Belong

I joined for acceptance,
I joined to belong.
It was my only bright
option in this world of right and wrong.
I don't know the stranger who I'm forced to call "Dad."
My reflection in the bathroom mirror
has been the only stable role model I've ever had.
Momma's too tired from work to be interested in my life,
most of the time she's too busy being a substitute in the sack,
for some other man's wife.
My brother's and sisters are always complaining
about not having enough to eat.
Peanut butter is the closest thing our kitchen has to meat.
School was my prison, my cage from nine to three,
where I was constantly bombarded with homework by the enemy.
The elite in society label me as part of a lost generation;
never once accepting me
as a victim of a trickle down economic nation.
Hence, they will never know how this "street rat" feels.
They will never know why I'm so willing to steal.
No more starving, no more school,
no more thoughts of being afraid to die.
Now I fight with fist, rock, steel, or bullet for my piece of the pie.
Only my fellow warriors, my brothers,
know what I'm going through,
by their side, and alone, I am proud to display my colors true.
Yes, I am proud of my only option
in this world of few rights and many wrongs.
I joined for acceptance,
I joined to belong.

*T*wo forks are placed at the dinner table
where the master sits,
two knives are also set
at the dinner table,
and like the forks, they are unfit.
Their union to partake of the bread of matrimony
is founded in deceit.
Yet they believe that they are truly worthy
to be participants at the master's feast.
"It is natural for two of the same utensils to be used
to devour the meat!" they say.
It is utter discrimination to ask that our lifestyle
not be an active candidate for display."
Two knives rest side by side on the dinner table,
a lasting penance to a disease, which has no cure.
Mirrored by two forks that desire to procreate artificially
with no Y chromosome in store.
The master condones their actions on the menu,
his blessing of the cuisine is adamantly clear.
This is a meal, a covenant,
"that only" a knife and a fork is destined to share.

The Drink

I pour the drink; I place the cup against my lips.
I smell the tantalizing aroma;
I debate upon whether to take a sip.
Every fiber in my being longing for sweet intoxication,
but I just look dumbfounded at the glass,
trying to fight the sensation.
If I partake of this elixir,
then I won't be able to feel the pain.
Unbelievably lose the strength that I have gained,
and be unable to empty the cup down the drain.
I might "as well" threaten to shoot myself in the head
with a gun,
because my life will be over once the drinking has begun.
Should I pour another, and another,
until I've drowned all of my fears?
Be a slave to the bottle, a captive for the rest of my years.
My consolation residing in the premise
that it will help me to forget this aching in my heart,
and temporarily bury the jagged memories
that continue to tear it apart.
I pour a second drink,
debating aloud whether to take a sip.
I smell the tantalizing aroma
as I place the cup against my lips.
Every fiber in my being longing for sweet intoxication,
but I just look at the glass,
trying aimlessly to fight the sensation.

Apart

They took her away from me, they took away my heart.
No one should have the power to keep a
mother and her child apart.
I'm not an unfit mother; I would never hurt my baby girl.
Yet they took away my lifeline, they took away my world.
They expect me to turn my back; they expect me to walk away.
To leave a baby girl wondering why her mother gave her away.
I will never get her back; hence I will always be alone.
A barren lake with no water, no life to call its own.
So that is the reason why I'm jumping,
because only death can stop my pain.
Hopefully the memory of my passing
will be more than just a red spot, a bloodstain.
They took her away from me, they took away my heart.
No one should have the power to keep a mother and her child
apart.

Prelude to Abortion

I have the potential to have two hands,
and given the chance,
I'll have a fully developed brain.
Please don't listen to the doctors that are telling you
that I can't feel any pain.
I have a heart, I have a soul, but indelibly my future is not my own.
And unlike your leg, I am not considered as flesh of your flesh,
and as bone of your bone.
The scientific term for me is a zygote,
but your conscience knows me as a child, "your baby."
And by agreeing to have an abortion,
you have consented to murdering me.
Like an inanimate flake of dandruff, you quickly brush me aside.
Doesn't the biblical commandment "Thou shalt not kill"
also apply to the life that you bear inside?
As my frail body is crushed within the vacuum,
and I am intricately removed from your sight;
I hope that you will remember me in your prayers,
and when you go to sleep at night.

Strings

I am a puppet
controlled by strings of fear.
A wooden doll
that shows no remorse
and cries no tears.
I am married to the puppet master,
a slave to his hands.
Always pulled, always beaten,
if I dare to disobey his commands.
So I lie to friends,
and tell them that all is well.
Hoping that they believed my bruises
were conceived when I accidentally slipped and fell.
I am becoming used to the pain,
but there is something that I cannot ignore.
The fact that one day he will punch me too hard,
only to rise no more.
He is a good man; he doesn't mean to hurt me.
If only I were a better wife,
then he would always be happy.
Believe me when I say that I love him,
and yearn for the tender man in him that I miss.
Even though I don't know whether to expect
a slap, or a kiss.
I don't want my children to know of the death threats,
scars, and burdens that I've had to bear.
Because I would rather die than to see them become
puppets controlled by strings of fear.

Daddy's Game

I hate Daddy's game; I hate it every time we play.
Why does he stare and touch me that way?
Why does he have to constantly
rub my bare chest?
Actively volunteer to play "Doctor" with his little princess.
Why does his hand have to touch me where I pee?
Why do I have to feel his finger poking inside of me?
I can't keep what we do a secret for long.
Every thought in my head
tells me that this situation is wrong.
I love my father; he's the center of my world.
I don't want to hurt him; I want to be a "good girl."
I hate Daddy's game; I hate it every time we play.
Sometimes I just feel like running away.

I Begged Him to Stop

Am I over reacting, he didn't beat me up?
Why did he do it? I begged him stop!
I keep crying, have to keep lying,
convince the rest of the world that I am not dying.
I'm confused and distraught, does the pain ever go away?
Do I have to live with this nightmare day after day?
Will I ever have a normal relationship with a guy again?
Or will the hated memories of that date never end?
I trusted him, why did he do this to me?
I can't help feeling violated;
it was as if he had stolen my virginity.
Am I a bad person, am I destined to live in agony?
I don't deserve this;
I don't deserve what that bastard did to me!
He forced me,
even though he didn't beat me up.
I didn't lead him on, I begged him to stop!

Nightmare Of Eternal Black

I walk to the courtyard, hands secured behind my back.
Staring at the dangling rope
while envisioning a nightmare of eternal black.
My audience awaits my final performance;
I can see the vehemence in their eyes.
My family watches me in agony,
not quite prepared to tell me goodbye.
As the noose is tightened around my neck
I whisper to the most high a silent prayer.
I hope that "the Almighty" listens to a man like me,
as I tremble like a reed in fear.
Like many before me I witness the beauty of my final sunset,
and as the hood covers my face I prepare to take my final breath.
As the priest speaks, I wish that I could turn back the hands of time.
Drill sense, morality and reason into the young man
who had so readily committed such an unforgivable crime.
Beneath the dark shroud I grit my teeth
and shed my secret tears.
Shivering, as the wretched silence wages an unholy war
upon my ears.
Screaming for mercy as my body plummets downwards;
hearing my neck crack, and then snap.
Slightly feeling my feet wriggle in the air
as I behold a nightmare of eternal black.

The Suicide Zone

*L*ike an ice cream knocked off of its cone,
one slowly dissipates into the eye
of the suicide zone.
Ominous is the sound
like a stalker's silence on the receiving end of a telephone.
Dread is the pin drop of confidence
that the ear refuses to hear.
As thoughts of doom and gloom
imprison the restless mind in fear.
Every rope is an interlude to a potential hanging place.
Every rooftop is a jump away from a future loss of face.
Every kitchen knife is your friend,
if only you could truly welcome him in.
Religion cast aside, as it is written, "All men have sinned".
Drop the fridge or bed on your throat;
ram full speed at the wall with your head.
Soak your hands
and insert a plug in an electrical socket by your bed.
Physical trauma will result in minutes, maybe hours of pain;
a slit or two of the wrist will cover the carpet for years
with a bloodstain.
A gun is a swift sentence,
but can the quivering hand
squeeze the trigger tight.
Or mouth overdose with a handful of pills
and drift less painfully out of the light.
This is when a person crumbles like parched clay
or refines like coal into the hardest stone.
Flesh and blood impervious to the sound of breaking bone,
because words and sanity lose all meaning
in the eye of the suicide zone.

In the Alley by the Pavement

Suddenly he punched me,
followed by slap after slap.
Ripped my
undergarments with his knife,
and told me I was trapped.
Afterwards, he forced my legs wide (too wide),
though I struggled in vain.
Then he pressed my weaker hands
against the icy pavement,
and injected his fiery pain.
In and out, again and again, hit after hit,
scream after scream.
A body, a temple defiled, a mind severely scarred;
never to be the same.
In the stomach he kicked me,
and my face he slapped once more.
In the alley by the pavement,
I lay like a battered "whore".
So, today I still tremble
in the presence of any man,
no matter his size or shape.
Because they remind me,
each one reminds me;
of the night I was beaten and raped.

Emerge

*W*oman, emerge from his shadow;
take your rightful place in the light.
You don't need a man to complete you,
not even in the wee hours of the night.
Cast aside the blanket of financial security
that has your neck wrapped in a noose.
Choose to live your life
based upon your joy and fulfillment;
end his cycle of mental abuse.
The sex isn't worth the tears
that frequently fall upon your pillow sheet.
The status isn't worth the black eye
that you console with frozen meat.
He doesn't appreciate you, but a substitute alone won't do.
Like an arrogant chef he has to have his cake and eat it too.
People will never understand why your love,
your dependence on him blinds your open eyes.
They can only behold a battered flagship
floating aimlessly on a sea of broken lies and faulty alibis.
Look deep within your soul
and embrace the innocent girl you once knew.
Remember her aspirations, her ideals, and her standards;
and make them a part of you.
Don't let the devil constantly steal your joy
like a thief in the night.
Woman, emerge from his shadow
and take your rightful place in the light.

*O*ne spreads the white powder on the glass
and prepares to take a sniff.
Another lights the glass pipe,
watches the smoke curl
and slowly takes a whiff.
If this were a song then these words would be the refrain.
Another lost soul tries to numb the pain.
One inserts the only bullet, spins the empty chamber,
points the nozzle at his head and squeezes the trigger.
As another's words slur, eyes dilate, and hand quivers
as she opens a next bottle of liquor.
Another has a knife, a bottle, or a pistol in hand
in preparation to steal and plunder.
Another walks the streets day after day,
seeking no shelter (no home) to sleep under.
Another ties the strap around her shoulder,
flicks the tip with a finger and sticks the needle in.
While another places his rent money
and next month's paycheck on the gambling table
hoping this time to win.
Another opens up her third pack for the day
frantically searching for a "light."
Another kindles his anger like a flame
and blames his troubles on everyone "white."
Another spreads her leg for the doctor
and hopes that her soon to be deceased unborn child
feels no pain.
Each one is a lost soul, each using a different method,
each one trying to numb the pain.

Shells
Of
Passion

The Bracelet

I wish to be the bracelet
wrapped around
your wrist.
Always near to you,
touching you,
knowing that you won't ever resist.
Yours to twist, yours to stroke,
and hopefully yours to hold.
To play an active part in your life,
a love as precious as gold.
To dangle at your side,
to feel your pulse rate soar.
To be comforted by your body heat;
by your side forevermore.
If I could be
your most precious possession,
my heart would feel eternal bliss.
My lady, I wish to be the bracelet
wrapped around
your wrist.

My Heart Won't Rest

*A*n eaglet,
longing to leave
the safety of the nest.
I try to forget what we shared, but my heart won't rest.
One more step is all I require to fall from on high.
To fall in love with another and allow my feelings for you to die.
But every time I look down I hear a familiar pounding sound;
that instilled fear, that without you, I will crash into the ground.
I spread my wings, time and time again,
attempting once again to fly.
One more step is all I require
to fall from on high.
Closing my eyes,
unable to ignore
the symphonic beat that jests.
Trying hard to forget what we shared, but my heart won't rest.

Candle

This candle still burns brightly for you,
and this heart still yearns
for that first love true.
And even though some of the memories
have been consumed during the years;
this light continues to shine,
even though the passion may have disappeared.
As the wax melts and the wick gradually fades away,
this beacon continues to persevere day by day.
And even though I have learned to love, respect,
and trust someone new.
This candle, my candle, still burns brightly for you.

The Moon

I stare out the window, eyes aglow,
gazing at the moon;
and I know that someplace,
somewhere,
you will be looking at it soon.
I hope that the same moonlight
that touches my heart
is somehow touching you,
loving and comforting you with its radiance, as I long to do.
I wish I could be the moon, and be able to see your gorgeous smile.
Have the power to capture your eyes and dreams,
for even a little while.
How I envy the moon;
that can so blatantly embrace you with care.
Yet, my heart is content,
knowing that it is this same moon
that we share.

Sparkling Like Embers

Eyes sparkling like embers, face as brilliant as the sun;
there is a burning in my heart,
and it's telling me that you are the one.
For the first time in many years I look through the eyes of a child.
The slightest thought of you is driving my imagination wild.
These eyes, your eyes, peer through this woman
to her very soul.
I try so hard to keep my hands off of you,
but temptation is taking its toll.
I hear the angels singing in chorus every time you smile.
Someday I hope to hear them again,
when I await your royal presence at the end of a chapel aisle.
My dear, in my heart you are second to none.
And as I peer into your eyes sparkling like embers
I know that you are the one.

Denied Water

*L*ike a plant being denied water, I am starting to die.
Baby, please come back to me before
my leaves are too dry.
I'm shriveling in my loneliness, a shadow of the man you once knew.
Falling apart with twigs of guilt, crumbling to pieces without you.
Waiting, anticipating the inevitable wind of return,
to tear away the rotten bark, that dead flesh from a love spurned.
The sun is now my enemy, a scorching reminder of my pain.
It's a heart that burned too vigorously,
and soon the relationship it nurtured will be slain.
These roots are strong, but I can't hold them steadfast alone;
eventually I will not be able to combat the winds of doubt
on my own.
Like a plant being denied water, my leaves are parched and dry.
Woman, please come back to me,
because without you I will surely die.

He Broke the Mold

*P*recious are diamonds, pearls, silver and gold.
But when God made you my dear,
he broke the mold.
The Almighty Father
must have spent the latter half of the sixth day
adding his finishing touches to you.
Needing to rest on the Sabbath day
after creating an almost perfect being of reason and virtue.
My lady, the blazing sun takes time to admire your beauty
because it knows that you are godsend.
A blessing to every fortunate man
whom you deem worthy to call your friend.
Herald angels marvel at your grace,
nightingales sing about your persona in their songs.
In the eyes of a child and this adult, you can never do wrong.
You are the purified essence of woman,
a magnificent treasure to behold.
Darling, when God made you he broke the mold.

Near to your heart

Near to your heart, like a pot of boiling water to a flame;
bubbling over for you with affection,
professing my love for you in clouds of steam.
Delighting in each line,
and each curve of your lovely face;
fortunate to be breathing the same air space.
Lady, my spirit overflows with joy and affection.
Every moment touching you is another sweet sensation.
Beloved, the sound of your voice is the highlight of my day.
Our memories are like scripture, they will never fade away.
And even though time and distance may keep us apart,
this man who loves you, and only you,
will always be near to your heart.

Tiptoeing in the air

My dear, you are my queen,
you are my lover,
you are my best friend.
You are my only, you are godsend,
and you will be my final thought before "the end."
Beloved, few men know the pure joy
of tiptoeing in the air;
to levitate body and soul when their companion appears.
To crumble like a mountain top
whenever pink bridges meet.
To sip lips of honey
while marveling at the way
her honeycomb tastes so sweet.
To exchange ideas and dreams upon clear clouds of desire;
to experience constant daylight in another person's eyes,
and be lifted spiritually higher.
To bask in the ebony beauty
and persona of the silver moon;
to laugh with the wind of devotion like a fallen flower,
and never be alone.
To have dropped weakly to their knees,
asking her to say 'yes' once more.
To kiss that angel of mystery time and time again,
and feel a burgeoning heart soar.
To die in her peaceful embrace
and be resurrected by the exhilarating warmth of her stare.
Few men are as fortunate as I to know the joy
of tiptoeing in the air.

Tender

Soft, so utterly soft
are your
sensuous supple
lips.
Tender, so tender
with each gentle, precious sip.
My lady; how the divine scent of you
clings tightly to me.
With a sweet aroma
that can only be defined as heavenly.
Empress, I am yours to obey,
to inspire, and to mesmerize.
Each tingle down my spine
is triggered by your champagne eyes.
Many men will want to drink
from the cup that is you.
Profoundly honored am I to say
that I am one of the astute few.
I can barely breathe in
without being reminded of your soothing touch.
Compounded by the thundering sound
of my heartbeat reverberating in my ears
as the blood below begins to rush.
Soft, so undeniably soft are your precious lips.
Tender, so tender,
that I would give my soul for one blessed kiss.

Beach
of
Beauty

Tanya

I am never too far to say that I love you
Tanya.
I am never to far away
to say that I care.
If you were a wandering star, beloved,
I would be on a comet trying to get there.
I always hoped that I would meet a woman
who was almost heavenly.
Lady, your presence in my life
has turned that prayer into reality.
Today, I am a plane ride away,
regrettably many miles away from your charm;
but soon there will be a sweet tomorrow
when I will be able to embrace you in my arms.
This is where my thoughts are;
this is also where my heart wishes to be,
wrapped tenderly in your arms like a newborn baby.
Tanya, I'm never too far to say that I miss you,
Tanya, I'm never too far to commemorate
this bond that we share.
If you ever need me woman,
seek the center of your heart,
and I will be there.

Simone

Simone;
when I've
forgotten
all of the rest,
trying desperately
to cling to memories true,
(of you) the best.
When I've experienced it all,
and there is nothing more;
within the many stars that twinkle,
your sparkling eyes I will adore.
When I'm at the end of the trail
and my faculties are few;
I will dwell on these special times,
be comforted by your smile once more,
and remember you.
When the roses rooted in friendship and respect eventually fade
and life's light grows dim,
leaving me shivering in death's evil shade.
This poem I wrote proves that even then,
I will never be alone.
Until my final sigh; it will always be
Simone.

Darlyne

*T*here is a sumptuous woman
who defines the word
"queen".
Who cowers from the limelight, remaining virtually unseen.
Trying to be a common person,
repudiating her claim to royalty.
But it is a hopeless endeavor
when her grandeur is as conspicuous as her beauty.
Such charm, such elegance,
has compelled many men (even me) to blatantly stare.
And although we covet her eyes, her smile;
it is her wit, and her demeanor we fear.
Indeed, one can always tell
when one is in the presence of a queen.
All hail, all hail, all hail, to the majesty of Darlyne.

Vashti

I was drawn to her eyes like a lemming to the sea.
Totally drawn to the startling smile and
enchanting beauty of Vashti.
Always wondering to myself at how long
the mystic attraction to her body would last.
Trying to escape her charms before another spell is cast.
But there is no magic except for the illusions of grandeur
in my mind.
For such a divine young woman could never be
so demeaning and unkind.
Intoxicated by her laugh, overpowered by her glowing face,
mystified by her movements,
especially when she walks with such grace.
That's when I realized that I never wanted my heart to be free;
because I have bewitched myself into falling
head over heels in love with Vashti.

Butter

I call her "Butter", but I am the one who melts.
To hold her in my arms for a few seconds,
I would risk my sanity, my health.
It is pure ecstasy to experience her soft skin and supple lips.
A tear of joy sheds from my eyes
when I watch her swing her vivacious hips.
She is so unbelievably sexy, and so devastatingly fine,
that a mere wink causes hot tingles to run down my spine.
For a minute she makes me feel that I could fly;
magically soaring high like an eagle,
until she bids me good-bye.
She is definitely a member of God's angelic host,
and someday I hope to have a woman like "Butter"
to spread on my toast.

Karen

I hear the wind across the shore,
it calls out a name.
Her name is the ocean's call,
and it is always the same.
Karen, belonging to a giver of joy,
a harbinger of happiness.
Karen, a woman who overflows like a fountain
with warmth and tenderness.
A goddess who transforms the dreary gray skies
into an expectant blue.
Who has taught me things about myself
that I never believed were true.
How I wish with all my heart
to be by Karen's side;
but all I have to comfort my lonely body
is the incoming tide.
So I listen to the wind across the shore
as it calls out Karen's name,
and even though my wish
can never come true,
I will always have Karen
in my memories and my dreams.

*M*y dear, God introduced me to you,
and you unveiled to me
a holy treasure.
An everlasting love
beyond the walls of pain and pleasure.
A sanctuary of joy
where my loins may find eternal rest.
A tabernacle where I can sacrifice
the robes of loneliness.
You are my fountain;
I quench my thirst from your heart-rending dew.
In your watery reflection the spirit of an angel
has revealed itself to me in you.
And I will drink forever,
bound by the covenant that God has set;
to see my nature rise in your eyes
and experience bliss in your sunset.
The bed is undefiled, all I have is yours to take;
to wash in passions basin,
and purify in heaven's wake.
Woman, God introduced me to you,
and you unveiled to me a holy treasure.
An everlasting love
beyond the walls of pain and pleasure.

Dark Waters
Of
Despair

The Heartbreak that Never Ends

One romance
after another,
never just a short
love affair.
Month after month of trust and devotion,
resulting in year after year of despair.
Constantly giving one's all,
only to get less and less in return.
Continuously starting the fire,
and always getting burned.
Every time the flame goes out,
apparently the story lives on.
Each page, each line,
depicting a relationship forlorn.
The main character I know too well,
he visits me in the mirror everyday.
Sometimes I wish
that I were able to skip a few pages
(The plot I would betray).
It seems that I've been reading
this particular chapter
over and over again!
Instead of this being deemed the book of life,
it should be called
the heartbreak that never ends.

Reef of Rejection

*L*ike a bottle
she was tossed upon
the reef of rejection.
A fool to have given away her trust,
and thus her protection.
So blind as to wear her heart upon her sleeve.
sOnly to watch it shatter against the rocks
when he told her to leave.
Upon that shore of self-pity only shards of contempt remain,
angry pieces of broken glass sharpened by her pain.
Eager to convey injury to any unsuspecting soul who comes along;
all because the one she confided in did her wrong.
Destroyed is the loyal vessel that was once overflowing with
affection.
Like a bottle
tossed upon the reef of rejection.

White Flag

oday, I show my white flag; today I surrender all.
Today, I shed a crystal tear
in honor of a house that is destined to fall.
I can't believe that it is over;
I can't believe this is the end.
We have written the final chapter,
we have given our final respects to a departed friend.
Years of joy, disappointment and romance
have traumatically come to a close.
Lost is the fragrance, withered are the petals of yesterday;
dead is the rose.
Bound is the book,
with no acknowledgement of the author's plight.
Sealed with a hug, not a kiss,
by two characters that have given up the fight.
Branding a white flag on its cover, for the entire world to see.
A lasting token of respect for a departed friend;
and a eulogy for you and me.

The Woman in My Dreams

Sometimes I wake up in a cold sweat calling out your name.
You are the one, the woman in my dreams.
By my bedside I see a pretty picture in a frame,
but it doesn't wink at me, so it doesn't feel the same.
It will never be as satisfying having you near.
Or as soothing as the sound of your sweet voice
whispering in my ear.
This plush pillow and cotton blanket
cannot comfort me from this cold;
I ache for your tenderness, I long for you to hold.
A phone call only reassures me that you are thinking of me as well.
Girl, everyday, every moment without you is a living hell.
I feel a bit of heaven every time I receive your perfume laced letters,
but the stroke of your hand, that gentle caress
will always be better.
I never realized how dependent I was until you came,
because you are the one, the woman in my dreams.

Play Another Sad Song

Play another sad song, so that I may forget.
Forget the love we shared;
forget that our sun has set.
Let me think in disillusionment
that someone else is hurting more than me.
Allow me to gain some solace in each verse of empathy.
Every word is a hole that I cannot fill.
Every adjective is a wave that threatens to drown my will.
Bear with me as I shed a few tears for a broken heart.
Closing my eyes tightly in order to recount the precious moments
of a commitment that has fallen apart.
And when I feel that my future has crashed severely
against denials rocky shore;
play another sad song
so that this vessel may hurt some more.

Oh the Kiss, How It Stings

What happens when the tongue grows tired
and the hands grow cold?
When your dashing frog prince
is no longer fit to behold?
Oh the kiss,
how it stings;
as that once sweet breath repels.
Welcome arms cringing in despair
as a loyal heart rebels.
When the thought of being together
is the furthest from your mind;
and the scales of passion peel away
to shock the blind?
Utter contempt and disgust
for the love, the man you once adored.
A relationship crucified by a woman
who cannot go through the motions anymore.
Thus many a headache comes to pass,
when the sex call rings.
As that once sweet breath repels;
oh the kiss,
how it stings.

I'm Not Made of Stone

I'm not made of stone;
Lord knows I can feel.
I melt, I move and
I bend like bars of steel.
Like any heterosexual man
I'm attracted to you like a Peruvian bee to a flower.
Your seductive power radiates a shower
that breaks me down with each passing hour.
But I've got to be strong, I can't throw true love away;
can't allow the winds of confusion
to force me to stray.
A part of me is wavering
like a man on a ladder about to lose his grip.
This man, someone's husband
would risk it all for the taste of your lips.
Woman I am unable to resist
your sensuous charms on my own.
So I ask you this favor, please leave me alone.
I have a solid marriage and I have a happy home.
But both will turn dust
once I partake of your enticing honeycomb.
Your wit, your grace, your tantalizing sex appeal;
evoke me to melt, to move, to bend like bars of steel.
This is the hardest decision I have ever known.
Woman, help me; Lord forgive me;
I'm not made of stone.

No more days to tell you how much
I love you.
No more days
to tell you how much
I care.
I should have told you but I never did.
Now I can't
because you are no longer here.
How do I live without my soul;
and beguile my mind not to lose control?
Honey, I love you so much right now,
but you will never know.
It just hurts so much having to let you go.
It would have been easier
if you had walked out the door.
Its utter torture
not being able to see you,
or touch you anymore.
No more days to tell you how much
I love you.
No more days to tell you how much
I care.
I should have told you, but I never did.
Now I can't,
because you are no longer here.

All I Feel Is Air

At night
that's when it really hurts,
when my life is filled
with despair.
Because every time I reach out to touch you,
to kiss you,
all I feel is air.
You said that you needed to do this on your own.
That was the night you left me,
left me to lie alone.
Darling, I will always love you,
even when you are dead and gone.
It's this precious love,
this bond that we share,
that keeps me holding on.
But you are not dead,
just somewhere far, far away.
And since you've left me,
I've been missing you everyday.
Someday my bed will be warm again,
and hopefully on that "someday"
you will be there.
But for now, when I reach over to touch you,
to kiss you,
all I feel is air.

Waves
of
Ecstasy

The Friction

*Y*oung lovers in heat,
there is something
you need to know
about that "safe sex message,"
"the jimmy,"
and "the physical flow."
"The rubber" wasn't meant to be 98% effective against foreplay.
Only abstinence and caution can keep those worries away.
One doesn't need to be a scientist
to disagree with this prediction.
Not even a garbage bag can stand up to "the friction."
Don't be so quick to brag about using only "the cap"
for protection.
It's only guaranteed if you adhere specifically to the directions.
Don't have so much faith in "the glove" adventurous one,
because there is no turning back once conception has begun.
If you are relying solely on "the latex," pray that it doesn't burst,
because at least one out of ten times you can expect the worst.
Read between the lines, the directions,
and evaluate exactly what the statistics say;
and realize that the condom was not made to be 98% effective
against foreplay.

No Gun In Sight

Shot in the heart, no gun in sight.
Struck by an invisible bullet
that is quicker than light.
Bleeding with lust, keeling over with anticipation.
Blind, dumb and deaf to any realistic sensation.
Maybe it was the way the sunlight
reflected from her eyes.
Maybe it was the way her skirt rode up her thigh.
She should have a safety catch attached to her smile,
a warning label plastered on her curvy profile.
When the almighty was blessing women with beauty
he gave her too much.
Totally lethal is the only way to describe her touch.
I am intellectually dead, fully aware of my plight.
Shot in the heart with no gun in sight.

My Master Key

Girl, my master key will open and reveal to you
those feelings that you have
suppressed inside.
In and out,
turning and twisting at each lock
until you are satisfied.
There is no combination too dear or safe too hard to "crack."
For patience, energy, and passion are a few characteristics
that these tender loins do not lack.
I've helped you open that ultimate door,
and I will continue to persevere hard at work
if you still crave for more.
Sensations, emotions, and a climax,
that you never believed were true;
released by my master key,
no longer locked securely within you.

You Shouldn't Have to Beg

A man like you shouldn't have to beg for affection;
when this woman who stands before you
is willing to give it without question.
You don't even have to ask for my admiration.
In this cup you will not find a single ounce of hesitation.
Pour me out; don't tease those lips with a sip.
Partake of all of me from shapely hip to hip.
With this body you won't need a plastic straw.
I will never be the one to tell you to withdraw.
Fill me completely where there exists emptiness;
and I will comfort you with love and tenderness.
Cast aside the confused vessel
that serves you with rejection.
A man like you shouldn't have to beg for affection.

Peel

eel me;
peel me until you
can peel no more,
open my lunch box and devour all that I have in store.
Darling my wheat is fresh and my soup is piping hot.
My sauce is sweet and tangy if you touch the right spot.
Dip my cherry like a cookie in milk and eat it "all up."
Place your tongue deep inside and sip my simmering cup.
Like a tangerine I am ready to be separated and plucked.
To feel your sleek lips and be tenderly sucked.
Juices flowing, body wet to the core.
Peel me; peel me until you can peel
no more.

One Last Kiss Goodnight

*O*ne last kiss goodnight.
Arms wrapped
around your
torso tight.
Feet seemingly hovering over the ground.
Two hearts beating in unison being the only sound.
Hands caressing gently, lips physically interlocked.
Tongues whipping to and fro, legs in a passionate gridlock.
The sweet mixture of salivary juice;
the innocent bucking of teeth.
The savory euphoria of togetherness forged by body heat.
A soft silent peck smothering a mouth that is glistening wet.
Wanton eyes transfixed upon each other
as if marveling at the sunset.
Two hands drifting apart like shadows resisting the morning light.
Followed by a tender embrace, a fleeting kiss,
and the final bid goodnight.

You Never Told Me

You never told me that you were gambling my future away.
You kept your secret to yourself as we lay.
I wanted my first time to be natural;
I wanted no sensations to be left aside.
To fulfill my dreams I needed to feel the intensity of your volcano
erupt its lava within my inside.
I trusted you with my dreams and emotions.
I gave you a partner willing to express total devotion.
I opened up my secret garden to you,
to cover with adoration like the morning dew.
During all the heart felt conversations and late night talks,
during all the foreplay on the sofa and the romantic walks;
you took all this body had to give.
You never once mentioned that you had been tested positive!
You never told me that you were physically sick.
You didn't even offer to adorn "the plastic."
You never told me that you were gambling my future away.
You kept your secret to yourself as we lay.

Wrap Me

*W*rap me up in your arms,
if only for tonight.
Tie my feelings in
bows of glee
and pull my body tight.
Read the label of my eyes
and entertain your mind.
Sense this precious treasure within,
and marvel at the riches that you will find.
This Yuletide season I promise
to present myself to you anew.
I am even willing to let you
take a peek before Christmas
if you want me to.
Gently open me up,
moving slowly from bottom to top.
Don't hold a single touch back;
don't allow your soothing hands to stop.
Passionately embrace this "one"
who loves you, and rapture me with care.
Partake wholly of my gift of love
which is yours to unwrap and enjoy
at this special time of year.

To Burn

I didn't plan this meaty encounter, we met by chance.
Igniting a torrid love affair sautéed in romance.
All I wanted was to feel the fire
that fondles again;
to burn inside and out with a flaming passion
that never ends.
To be irresistible and pampered
for at least one night.
To realize that someone is truly listening to my concerns
as he holds me tight.
To be more than a wife and a mother for part of the day.
To sigh in awe at the stroke of another person's touch,
virtually carried away.
To softly coo like a pigeon at the intensity
of another person's kiss.
To no longer be taken for granted
in the sea of matrimonial bliss.
To feel special and appreciated as a queen should.
To tingle from skin to core, knowing that the love is good.
To feel sexually attractive, body and soul once more.
To experience the element of danger
from bed sheet to kitchen floor.
To know that the urge, the need for climax
will be continually met.
To attain a measure of ecstasy that I will never forget.
To inhale with each firm thrust,
to exhale with each stimulating release.
To burn inside and out, every fiber of my being at peace.

Tossed

*L*ike a salad
you allowed
your emotions
to be tossed,
because you refused to keep your legs crossed.
How much dressing did he coat with his words
before he ventured down low?
How long did it take for him to nibble
down to your garden below?
When you were stripped
clean of your undergarments,
why did you not abstain?
Why did you allow him to poke his fork
into your lettuce green?
Why did you not protect your tomatoes
from the juices that were destined to flow?
Now in you, another unwanted crop is about to grow.
Mothered by a used meal whose young freedom
and college years have been tossed.
All because you refused to keep your legs crossed.

Shoals
of
Thought

Checking Account

*Y*ou are just another checking account to me,
one more quick investment
in my financial history.
Not a fixed sum, but a pretty face with a sexy body,
a bodacious backside, caramel eyes and luscious lips.
An open teller anxious to accept my deposit slip.
An overnight transaction that I deemed profitable to earn.
A selected short-term prospect with minimal return.
Each deposit, each capital gain,
succumbing you to my will.
Each cash flow a capitalistic thrill.
Upon loss of interest I will tactfully seek divestment.
Permanently withdraw all funds
and seek a more profitable investment.
Utter remorse, without pity for leaving an empty "kitty."
Because you are just another checking account to me.

The Sword

A sharp two-edged sword,
eager to protect and to take.
A weapon usually
withdrawn when
honor and duty are at stake.
The flash of the metal is the
foolhardiness of my pride.
Concealing the truth that I adamantly try to hide.
Drawing closer and trusting deeper with each thrust.
Each cut revealing something more lascivious than lust.
Disabling all defenses with each vicious slice.
My future and my life being the ultimate sacrifice.
Stabbing at the persona from the very start.
All for the thrill of piercing the vigilant heart.
Body numb, and mentally detached by the sensation
of cold penetration.
Damned by the sword that
runs me through
with adoration.

The Spider

Beware of the spider, beware I say,
because we will all come
face to face with him
someday.
Stay away from the spider, though many are taught,
they dare to play with this predator,
and are eventually caught.
Mostly prisoners of circumstance, victims of fate;
made to wait like lambs to the slaughter,
penance being too late.
Suspended in despair; dangling upon very thin lines.
Trapped by curiosity; condemned by a web so fine.
Such a sticky situation, for all an awful way to die;
but resistance is futile when you are the fly.

Paint

He paints his wall,
he paints it with care.
Ignoring that the
sunlight has
almost disappeared.
He paints his wall,
his job being almost done.
The paint is fresh,
but gone is the sun.
Inside the house he goes
to wipe his speckled hands clean;
unaware that the paint on the wall
is being washed away
by the rain.

A Hanger

*T*hrow away the robe;
the man you once
knew is gone.
Don't be like a hanger, still holding on.
You will never sail like him if your anchor
remains submerged beneath "the blue."
He's found another port to dock at,
he's found someone new to pursue.
Desist from clinging, to the memories of old
like lint to a frock.
Still fondling your midsection, recounting
the many ways he used to pick your lock.
A frigid pillow, lost and alone,
with no cheek to warm its side.
Too plush, too pregnant,
too anxious to be his bride.
Still hoping that he will one day
drift to your shore:
Place a ring on your finger, be a father
to the child you have in store;
accompany you down the aisle,
over the threshold and through the bedroom door.
Woman, throw away the robe;
the love you once knew is gone.
Don't be like a hanger,
still holding on.

Island

Blues

The Bahamas

*L*ook at the enchanting blue waters, behold my majesty.
Smell the salty air; know that you are next to me.
Taste the cool whimsical sea breeze,
my own gentle arms you embrace.
Touch the sparkling silver sands,
and stroke my ebony face.
Listen to the boastful waves (my heartbeats),
as they crash against the shore and fizzle away.
Know me as **Bahamas**;
a sacred love to enjoy and treasure
everyday.

Bahamian Time

*A*n English man would declare such apathy a crime,
but to the local businessman,
it's a norm to be working on
"Bahamian time."
To the Japanese executive who never likes to be late,
he better fold his arms, bite his nails, and just wait.
Twenty minutes later, and two flips of a dime,
the island businessman arrives on "Bahamian time."
To be punctual for the afternoon,
one has to catch the breakfast flight.
Two delays, maintenance check, and then hold on tight.
But there is one thing that Bahamians see
as a punctilious crime,
that is not being able to leave one's job everyday
exactly at quitting time.

There Go the Lights Again

There go the lights again, when will this parody ever end.
If I were a business downtown,
the generator must be my friend.
Every other day I witness the loss of electrical power.
Sometimes it comes for twenty minutes at a time,
sometimes not for hours.
I used to blame my misfortune on the thunder and the rain.
But they were not at fault;
something else was the efficacy of my pain.
A government Neanderthal
who manifests chaos without paying any cost.
Generating insufficient power to my home
in order to facilitate a place named after a paradise lost.
For the average Nassauvian, the blinking alarm clock,
the candle or flashlight must be their friend.
There go the lights again, when will this parody ever end.

Someone

(Election Day 1992)

Someone will be mourning in the end,
because there is always a loser
in an election my friend.
To be able to vote for our leaders
is an opportunity, a Godsend;
a chance to dictate whether pain or prosperity
will be around the bend.
In time, the disappointment and disgust
spawned by the results will mend.
But someone, yes someone,
will be hurting in the end.

Food for the Soul

Cowbells ringing in the air, toes start to dance.
As the procession comes closer,
legs begin to prance.
Torsos rocking erratically,
arms trembling from shoulder to thumb.
Bodies vibrating to the rhythm
of the pulsating goatskin drum.
Eyes marvel at the kaleidoscope of colors
of crepe paper, newspaper,
cardboard, beads and cloth.
Hips gyrate slightly to and fro,
hands swaying from spot to spot.
Followed by constant jigging, weaving,
and bobbing of heads
to the hypnotic beat.
Every soul who has a bleacher seat
is standing on their feet.
The music is taking over;
as a parade of laughter, shouts and smiles abound.
Tourists and locals alike
are intoxicated by the exotic Junkanoo sound.
The melodic scream of the brass sings, the whistles chirp,
and the group chants take control
All hail Bahamian music;
a sweet musical aphrodisiac
which is pure harmonic food for the soul.

How Long

*H*ow long will I have to walk the streets of Nassau in fear?
Wondering if tomorrow's broadcast
will highlight the loss of someone I hold dear.
Attend a club in the evening
without being searched for a hat or a weapon;
illegally run the red light in the wee hours of the night
because my life may be threatened.
When will I be able to enjoy a reggae or rap concert
without having to avoid a fight?
Feel secure enough to walk down Bay Street and Western Espio-
nage
in the moonlight.
Read the Tuesday newspaper without seeing an article
about someone being robbed, stabbed or shot.
Or read an editorial about a thief being prosecuted
a few months after being caught.
When will drivers who do not signal be charged
and forced to pay a fine?
Why do white-collar criminals attain public redemption
without serving prison time?
When will the politicians, lawyers and judges
implement a proper and swift legal system?
How many bars, dogs, security guards, and motion detection
systems
must the private sector purchase to sugarcoat this problem?
When will our present government look beyond the sun,
the international economy; and set us free?
When will they castrate the rapist, lock up the drug dealers/

This Land

This land,
she is my land,
this land,
she is your land.
From Inagua's great banks
to Abaco's shimmering white sand.
From the first day you cried
after being plucked like a yellow elder
from your mother's womb.
Until the day you are swept above San Salvador
in the arms of God from a dreary tomb.
Your blood is the aquamarine
that breathtakingly stains the shallow sea.
Along with your British heritage
the golden sand bears footsteps of your precious history.
Black is the heart, the mind and the spirit of a nation
that you share.
Independent and world renowned,
fostered by the sweat and sincerity
of your forefather's prayers.
The hunger in your belly is instilled by the conch fritters,
guava duff or crab and dough that you feel like eating.
The rhythm of your soul is the Junkanoo
or rake-n-scrape beat you hear within.
Silver was the importance of our country's 25 year jubilee;
toasted with gin and coconut water, bursting with energy.
Every time you lift up your head
and see a flag raised on a pole
or a native hand;
be proud to be a Bahamian.
Be proud to know that "this land"
is your land.

About the Author

Sean Munnings (a.k.a. The Raga~Lover) was born in Nassau, Bahamas on December 26, 1973. He attended Queens College High School, and graduated from the College of the Bahamas with an Associate of Arts Degree in Banking. He furthered his education abroad at the University of South Florida where he acquired a Bachelor of Science Degree in Accounting and a Master's Degree in Finance. He later obtained a qualification as a Certified Public Accountant while working as an auditor at PricewaterhouseCoopers (formerly Pricewaterhouse). He is currently the Deputy Manager at Dartley Bank & Trust Limited , is a member of Toastmasters Club 7178 and resides in Nassau, Bahamas.